SAVING YOUR MARRIAGE

OVERCOMING INFIDELITY

I0171417

BY

SHERYLN MILLER

&

KATHY WATERMAN

PRINCIPLES PUBLISHING

Saving Your Marriage Overcoming Infidelity

First Published in 2015 by Principles Publishing

Principles Publishing
P.O. Box 85
Bridgeport, MI 48722

The authors may be contacted at the above address or the following:

principlespublishing@gmail.com

Photography by: Laura Quarry

ISBN-13: 978-0692461266

Special Thanks to Pastor Jack Steenbergh of Coleman Wesleyan Church

Table of Contents

Introduction

Many young women secretly think once they are married, everything will be perfect. However, this can be erroneous thinking if they are not mentally and emotionally prepared for the challenges marriage brings. When two people enter into a relationship they should know all about the other person's personal beliefs. Do they share the same goals? Do they like to save money or live for the moment and never save a dime? What happens when spouses do not share the same religious beliefs? What happens if your potential mate does not believe in God? Are you willing to give up your beliefs? Will you agree to go to separate churches? What happens if one person wants to have children and the other person does not? Are you prepared to love your spouse in sickness and in health? Being healthy makes things easy, but sickness may place a financial and emotional strain on your marriage. Is one partner easily distracted when a nice looking man or woman walks by, or does that person have eyes for only you? It is acceptable to comment about an attractive person, but do they make you uncomfortable with their comments and staring? Getting married is not going to change the person, so it is important that you can love their flaws along with their positive qualities.

It is important to remember that both partners have a part in the disintegration of a marriage. Everyone is busy with jobs, children, hobbies, and other responsibilities that pertain to daily living. Will you make time to focus on strengthening your relationship? Some families will set aside one evening a week to spend time with each other. Some have game nights, and others have movie nights. Having dinner together helps families draw closer as they communicate and share the day's events and happenings. It is important to learn to say no to extra activities or commitments when it is going to overstress the family.

Author Kathy Waterman remembers that before she and her husband were married, he said he would not marry her unless she agreed to go on a date with him once a week. She quickly agreed to his request. Who doesn't want to go out with their spouse and spend time with him? They followed through with this plan for several years. They also planned time away every year for their anniversary. It was fun looking for new places to go and spend quality time together. Usually, they found a hotel about an hour away, but a couple times they planned trips to Toronto, Canada and Cancun, Mexico. As time passed, it was harder to keep the promise. They no longer kept date night, and Kathy missed it. If they did get away, her husband's focus was on work or the farm. The meaning of date night was totally forgotten. Recently, they started making time for date night again. They went to Jamaica for their anniversary. They have been married thirty-four years now. Their marriage has had ups and downs, but they have been committed to honoring God and their wedding vows.

Divorce has become the easy way out when a marriage has lost its thrill. Some people have financial burdens and the stress of the debt causes fighting. The fighting leads to bitterness, and before you know it they are thinking about divorce. Divorce can happen for many reasons. My hope is that you can sit back and look at everything objectively. What are the benefits of staying together? How will it change your life if you divorce? Can marriage counseling help you work out your differences? Divorce should not be a rash decision, and you should be sure before making it final. Divorcestatistics.org states that 45-50% of first marriages end up in divorce, while 60-67% of second marriages divorce and 70-73% of third marriages end up divorced. Perhaps just knowing about the statistics will encourage you to seek ways to improve your marriage instead of starting over. Many people who have decided to get a divorce will tell you it is the worst thing they have ever gone through.

One may say marriage is a team sport because the husband and wife help each other emotionally, physically, and spiritually. This was God's plan, and it works if husband and wife are committed to loving God with all their heart and soul which results in unconditional love for each other.

The following account details the struggle of a couple whose marriage failed because of infidelity. Although it occurred in another country, it happens around the world.

Chapter 1
A Marriage in Trouble

Samantha and Tom accepted an overseas, or "expat," position. Wikipedia explains says, "An expatriate (often shortened to expat) is a person temporarily or permanently residing in a country other than their own citizenship. The term is often used in the context of professionals or skilled workers sent abroad by their companies."

When Samantha and Tom received their orders to move to Shanghai, China, there was excitement in the air. They were excited about moving to another country, but they were also sad they were leaving behind their family and friends. Many things were going through their minds. Samantha was hoping that the time away would bring them closer. Tom was hoping this would jumpstart his career and result in a promotion or two.

Moving to China brought many new challenges. The first was the language. Samantha found that by playing charades she could make herself understood and get what she wanted. Some of the people tried very hard to help, while others walked away. A calculator helped negotiate prices. They quickly learned to bargain for everything, which in time became a lot of fun.

The next problem was how to tell the driver where she wanted to go. Each expat has a personal driver, as they are not allowed to drive in China. This is a company rule designed to protect employees. Things we take for granted, like auto and health insurance, are handled very differently. If someone is involved in a car accident, the charges for the repairs are settled immediately on the scene. This isn't easy if you don't speak the language. If a person is injured, the responsible party must pay for all medical expenses and support the person until he or she recovers. If a person does not recover the party must support the person for rest of his or her life. It was a challenge to tell the driver to pick Samantha up at a certain time. It all depended on the language they spoke. To unite everyone, the government wanted everyone to speak Mandarin. However, The Chinese people speak many different languages. Tom and Samantha had a driver who spoke a mix of Mandarin and Taiwanese. If Samantha told him 12:00 P.M, he thought it was 2:00 P.M., this became a problem when she needed to be somewhere at a certain time. To solve the problem, she made up cards with the time in Chinese on one side and in English on the other side. By purchasing business cards printed in both Chinese and English, the destination problem became easier.

The third difference was a maid. Samantha lucked out and got a wonderful Aiya (in China all maids are called Aiya). She was a cheerful person and became part of the family. She cleaned the house, cooked supper, and helped with charity projects. The last barrier was where to shop. Fortunately, a lady in her husband's company called to see if she needed help. She showed her where to buy meat, rice, and specialty products at Australian or European stores. The rest could be purchased at Chinese grocery stores or fruit and vegetable markets.

Samantha and Tom had many challenges before settling into their home. All their clothing was lost for three days. They arrived in Shanghai, China at about 9:00 p.m., after traveling for eighteen hours straight. Their clothing did not make it with them. They now had to try to explain to the luggage department their luggage was missing. It was very difficult as they only spoke Chinese and Tom only spoke English. Tom and Samantha were not sure they were understood, or if they would ever see their luggage again. Thankfully, they remembered a man named Tony, he helped them when they were looking for a house. They called him to explain what happened. Tony promised to look into it and get back with them. On their third day in Shanghai, they finally received a call from Tony saying their luggage had been found and would be delivered soon. At 5:00 that evening Tom called Tony to tell him the luggage had not arrived. Tony called back to say the man with their luggage was three hours out of the city going the wrong way. They finally received their luggage around 10:00 p.m. that night and the rest of their belongings arrived six weeks later.

The days were long, and the nights lonely. Tom worked long days and nights as he was required to attend dinner meetings. Drinking was a common activity at the meetings. Samantha did not know prostitutes were at the restaurants. Prostitutes preyed on expat men as a source of income. Many businesses used prostitutes as a night's entertainment. The women come out and line up, the men pick out which one they want to wait on them for the night. She gets his drinks, food, and anything else he wants for the night. When it is time to go to the hotel, she goes with him. This is the business culture of China, and they do not feel there is anything wrong with it.

The first six months went by and instead of them growing closer they grew further apart. Tom had become so attracted to the women that he would tell his wife she revolted him, she was too fat and he couldn't stand being around her. He traveled to surrounding areas often for one or two weeks at a time. He went to places like India, South Korea, Taiwan, Thailand and other parts of China. These places all had similar customs. In Thailand he visited bars where all the women were totally nude. He became more and more immersed in their way of life. Tom began to forget his marriage vows. He also forgot about the Bible verse that says "Husbands ought to love their wives as their own bodies. He who loves his wife loves himself." (Ephesians 5:28)

One week, while Tom was gone, Samantha started feeling sick. She was listless, had a low grade fever, and a terrible vaginal growth. When Tom came home, Samantha told him about her symptoms. This is when he told her he had been with a prostitute. She had picked him up at a bar one night and had taken him to a massage parlor. He had used a condom, but it broke.

For the next six months they both went to many different doctors and were on many different antibiotics. At times they were on two to three different antibiotics. Shanghai did not have the technology or equipment to test what kind of infections they had, so it's a lot of guess work. It wasn't until a trip back to the U.S. that Samantha found out what IV antibiotic they both needed. They were lucky - the testing confirmed they were not HIV positive.

When a husband (or wife) forsake their wedding vows Satan beguiles them into thinking no one will find out, or that everyone else is doing it, so, "why not me?" When we lose sight of God's path, we get lost. We believe the lies Satan whispers to us. We become puffed up with pride. We lose. Thankfully God has Amazing Grace.

Samantha had made her own life through the American Women's Club (AWC), friends, volunteering, missionary work, and volunteering on committees at Church. Her volunteer work ranged from raising money for migrant schools to helping poor Chinese women learn a new trade so they can support themselves. Tom became more immersed in his job, late night meetings, teleconferences or going out with the guys. Samantha found out she couldn't even trust the women Tom worked with. They would tell him he had been married to his wife for too long, and he needed to divorce her. This would keep him young at heart. Men who go to China are often very naïve. They are not used to the attention the women give them. They get a big head and it doesn't get any smaller until they return home to the U.S. The Bible tells us to stay away from people who approach us with smooth talk and flattery because they are not serving Christ. They are doing so out of their own selfish needs or agenda. The passage goes on to say, "they deceive the minds of naïve people." (Romans 16:17-18)

Tom traveled often. What he didn't tell his wife was that he was traveling with the women he was training at work, the same women who wanted him to divorce her. He seemed to have a crush on one of his co-workers. Samantha said, he was always talking about her. He would talk about how cute she was, how she had this to say, how she did this or that, and how she has the cutest face. His deception continued.

Samantha and Tom attempted to work on their marriage. They tried marriage counseling with different counselors. Tom always tried to put all the blame on Samantha. He would talk about things that happened to her when she was much younger. Saying she had a certain problem because of her parents or her first husband. He would never talk about the problem at hand. Samantha tried to set guidelines with him and the counselor, saying "we are here because Tom was unfaithful. His actions are causing problems in our marriage, and I am having a hard time dealing with it." He seemed to think he was helping the prostitute by paying for her services, instead of hurting their marriage. Samantha also stated that if he kept sidetracking, she no longer wanted to continue the counseling sessions. It was like she was being assaulted all over again with no one to help her. Samantha finally decided to quit counseling and find her own personal counselor. Tom refused to get counseling on his own because he believed he did not have a problem.

One day Samantha was on the computer and was looking to see what websites her husband was looking at. She found many Chinese porn sites. This was so shocking and disturbing for Samantha that she called Tom to say she was leaving. It was like one more assault on their marriage. After discovering the pornography, Samantha gave Tom an ultimatum, that he see another counselor or she would go home. He agreed and saw another counselor during the rest of their stay in Shanghai.

They fought continuously, jealousy and distrust was always present. Tom continued to lie or omit information his wife wanted or needed to know. As Samantha figured out each lie, she mistrusted him even more. Up to the last few days of being in China she continued to learn more lies or omissions. Tom and Samantha returned home and continued to work on their marriage. Tom found a good counseling group to join and he seemed to make progress and finally apologized to his wife for what he put her through. Tom told Samantha he loved her and wanted to make their marriage work.

Samantha was happy for Tom that he seemed to feel at peace now. However, Samantha was not at peace. She was angry and hurt. Samantha did not know how to trust again, or give her heart to a man that had hurt her so badly. She knows that God says you have to forgive to be forgiven, but forgiveness was hard to find. Three years of mistrust had taken a toll on their marriage. She tried one more counselor, and joint counseling with her husband. Tom did not like the counselor and stopped going. They remain together and are working on their marriage. They have gotten pass the jealousy and mistrust. And Samantha is trusting that God will heal her heart as she learns to trust Him.

When you learn to trust God, He works miracles, "Because he himself suffered when he was tempted, he is able to help those who are being tempted." (Hebrews 2:18)

What Kathy found in China is that it doesn't matter who the couple is. The man could be geeky, ugly, fat, old, or bald. He could even be a church leader. Too often they have a girl on the side. She has personally seen too many marriages destroyed. The women use expat men to escape from a world of poverty. Many women don't want to work, and love is not a factor in most cases. The men have been primed, their egos enlarged and they feel as if they can do anything because of the compliments and attention the women give them.

One man brought his mistress to his home to meet his wife. He introduced her as a co-worker who needed to know where to shop. He asked his wife to help her out. Once the mistress knew everything her husband liked and where to shop, the wife was sent home and the mistress took her place.

Another man came home one day with a one way ticket for his wife back to the US. He gave her the ticket on a Friday, and he said she had better be on the plane on Monday. They had sold their home, cars, and everything they owned. He put all their money in his name and she returned home with nothing. She had no money and no home. I told her to get a good lawyer. For this reason, one party should not control all of the finances. Both need to be partners in financial matters. Find out where your money is being spent and where it is being invested. Is there money missing? You do not want to be left abandoned the way this poor woman was after working hard all her life.

What the Chinese women don't understand is the wives of these men are well educated. The women have sacrificed their careers so their husbands can advance in theirs. I have met women who were doctors, nurses, lawyers, teachers, and other professionals who have fallen into this trap. Never were the men thankful for their sacrifice. Instead their wives became unwanted baggage. Many send their wives and children packing without a second thought. The Chinese women wanted our life styles. They do not realize that once we are home we will go back to work, clean our own homes, do the yard work, and help with parents and grandchildren. No more will we have maids or drivers.

I have seen many men spend every penny they have on the women they meet. After all of the money is gone the women send them packing and move on to the next clueless victim.

In time, this eventually backfires on the men. I talked to a psychologist who is seeing some of the men who tossed their families aside for younger women. They are now finding out that after the sex becomes old that they have made a big mistake. The age difference is too big, and they have nothing in common. They don't speak the same language or have the same sense of humor. Most of these women don't have a high school education, much less a college education. When the man is a high executive, this is a big difference. What do you talk about after the party gets old, and you have absolutely nothing in common?

The men do not see that Satan is deceiving them and leading them to destruction. He tells them they deserve whatever they want. By the time their eyes are opened, they have broken every promise and vow they have ever made.

I know a smart and classy lady who experienced the sad betrayal we are discussing. She is a funny, well-educated, upper class, beautiful person. I say this because I want you to realize it doesn't happen to a particular class of women. No one was safe in China. She did a lot of charity work and was constantly busy helping others. They lived in China for about 5 years. One day her husband came home and asked for a divorce. She later found out he had been with so many prostitutes that he didn't even know how many he had been with, and now he wanted to marry his latest. This man is in his 60's and he married a 23 year old Chinese woman. His children were so hurt that they no longer talk to him. During his last trip home, he was busy gathering every penny he could get and moving it into another account with his name only. He had everything planned before asking for the divorce. I would say most women in their 60's would not expect their husband to leave them for a 23 year old. Can you imagine starting your life over now after you planned for retirement?

So what does the Lord God, creator of heaven and the universe say about such behavior? Scripture tells us God hates divorce. For the Lord God of Israel, says: "I hate divorce and marital separation and him who covers his garment (his wife) with violence. Therefore, keep watch over your spirit (that it may be controlled by My Spirit), that you deal not treacherously and faithlessly (with your marriage mate)." (Malachi 2:16 Amplified Version)

God knows if we do not watch over our spirit, if we do not allow ourselves to be controlled or influenced by His Holy Spirit we will follow the world's customs and divorce our spouses based upon selfish, sinful desires

God has plenty to say about marriage, divorce and even our sexual relationships. (Leviticus 20:10-22). Please note that most of the book refers to men but we know women fall into the snare of infidelity as well.

Chapter 2
Come Out From Among Them

The Holy Spirit cries out to men and women to avoid the world's bidding to pursue temporary pleasures. The Christian man or woman must get on the straight and narrow path. He or she must avoid the wide path that leads to the destruction of marriage and soul. The spirit of the world cries out with visual signs calling to individuals to get on the broad path of pleasure. The spirit of the world beckons us to come to it, to imbibe on the sweet pleasures of sin.

The streets of China are filled with massage parlors. Every day the newspapers advertise massages with "Happy Endings." The "happy endings" are temporary and will destroy a man's soul. Yet, the blind, gullible, and foolish men seek them. The advertisements are directed toward business men. They advertised "to your home in 30 minutes." You do not even have to leave the comfort of your own home!

Prostitutes are visible in every restaurant, hotel, and bar. You could be on a vacation in a five star hotel and they will call your hotel room at night. We have experienced them going door to door to get business at the hotels.

In the US, it's not quite as obvious. The casual flirt at the office or the business lunch or dinner often turns into something more than the parties initially desired.

The internet has made it much easier to cross the line from morality to immorality all in the privacy of your own home. You can lie to yourself and say it is harmless but if you are truthful, it is destroying your marriage.

Scripture tells us we can't have two lords. We will worship one and hate the other. You can't serve God and love your wife, while looking at pornography (idols/images of unsanctified men and women). Does your spouse know you think he or she is more important than anyone else? If not, you need to spend time investing in your marriage. A woman I know wrote on Facebook. "Came home to a spotless house, roses, a massage and a thank you card for being a great wife and mommy. Feeling loved." Now that is a man investing in his marriage!

Do you take your spouse for granted every day by living in fantasy land? It is time to turn your heart to the Lord and to your spouse, seeking forgiveness and restoration.

Chapter 3
God Attends All Weddings

Did you know God attends all weddings? He said in Malachi 2:14 that he was a "witness (to the covenant made at your marriage) between you and the wife of your youth, against whom you have dealt treacherously and to whom you were faithless. Yet she is your companion and the wife of your covenant (made by your marriage vows)."

When a man and woman exchange wedding vows, the vows are considered holy and sacred. They are a covenant performed in the presence of God. God's heart is grieved when a man decides to divorce or separate from his wife when she gets older because He remembers the ceremony and the covenant he made to love honor and cherish his wife until parted by death.

Making and breaking a covenant or vow before the Lord is very serious and potentially dangerous. Solomon said it is foolish to make a vow and then say it was a mistake. He asked why God should destroy the work of your hands because you failed to keep a vow. Perhaps the lack of success in life or work may be the result of not keeping marital vows.

Solomon reminds us not to let our mouths lead us into sin. He said, do not protest to the temple messenger, "My vow was a mistake, Why should God be angry at what you say and destroy the work of your hands?" (Ecclesiastes 5:6 Amplified)

Proverbs 2:17 speaks of a woman who forsook the husband of her youth and forgot the covenant of her God. Notice the verse said it is "the covenant of her God." John Gill says it is the, "covenant of God; not only because God is the author and institutor of marriage, and has directed and enjoined persons to enter into such a contract with one another; but because he is present at it, and is a witness of such an engagement; which, as it adds to the solemnity of it, makes the violation of it the more criminal."

Chapter 4
What Jesus said About Divorce

When you first read Jesus' response to the Pharisees question about divorce and remarriage, you might say what the disciples said, "that it's best not to get married!" (Matt 19:10) Because of the strict law on divorce and remarriage, the disciples said it was better not to marry.

It's best not to marry? According to scripture, if a person marries and divorces his or her spouse, except for sexual immorality, and they marry someone else he or she commits adultery. There are many married couples living in adulterous relationships today because according to scripture they are still married to their first spouse. How can this be? They are still married to their first spouse because God did not acknowledge or honor the divorce complaint when it was filed. He did not honor it because it was not based upon biblical statue. The law says that the wife must be guilty of adultery or fornication for the complaint to be valid. If she is not guilty of such, the complaint is thrown out and a divorce is not granted. The couple is still married. Therefore, if he or she marries another person they are considered adulterers and adulteresses because they are legally bound to another. This is serious because scripture tells us, adulterers and fornicators do not inherit the kingdom of God. At the coming of the Kingdom of God, in the New Jerusalem, the place where the streets are paved with gold, the adulterers are said to be outside the city. They are not allowed to come into the city to defile it.

There are exceptions to the rule such as physical violence. However, getting fat, falling out of love, getting old, not sharing the same goals or dreams, not making enough money, and so on are not biblical grounds for divorce.

Let's review the conversation between Jesus and the Pharisees:

Matthew 19:3   The Pharisees also came to Him, testing Him, and saying to Him, "Is it lawful for a man to divorce his wife for just any reason?"

Matthew 19:4   And He answered and said to them, "Have you not read that He who made them at the beginning 'MADE THEM MALE AND FEMALE,'

Matthew 19:5   and said, 'FOR THIS REASON A MAN SHALL LEAVE HIS FATHER AND MOTHER AND BE JOINED TO HIS WIFE, AND THE TWO SHALL BECOME ONE FLESH'.

Matthew 19:6   So then, they are no longer two but one flesh. Therefore, what God has joined together, let not man separate."

Matthew 19:7   They said to Him, "Why then did Moses command to give a certificate of divorce, and to put her away?"

Matthew 19:8 He said to them, "Moses, because of the hardness of your hearts, permitted you to divorce your wives, but from the beginning it was not so.

Matthew 19:9 And I say to you, whoever divorces his wife, except for sexual immorality, and marries another, commits adultery; and whoever marries her who is divorced commits adultery."

Matthew 19:10 His disciples said to Him, "If such is the case of the man with his wife, it is better not to marry."

Matthew 19:11 But He said to them, "All cannot accept this saying, but only those to whom it has been given:

The Pharisees used Deuteronomy 24:1, as legal permission to divorce their spouse for any reason.

Deuteronomy 24:1 "When a man takes a wife and marries her, and it happens that she finds no favor in his eyes because he has found some uncleanness in her, and he writes her a certificate of divorce, puts it in her hand, and sends her out of his house..."

In order to comprehend what Christ said, we need to understand that, during the disciple's time, men were divorcing their mates based upon their fleshly interpretation of the Law of Moses. Men would "put away" their wives for any reason. Commentator Matthew Henry says, "If she burned his food or did not fix his meal exactly the way he wanted her to. If she had a bad temper, if he saw someone prettier than his own wife, or if he was just tired of looking at her."

A woman could be married one minute and divorced the next. A Pharisee's wife could lose favor in his eyes quickly and easily. A man could see another woman he liked better, go before the Sanhedrin to obtain a certificate of divorce, take it to his wife, and she would be divorced. Jesus is clearly addressing the abuse of the law of Moses. He was getting to the heart of the matter; they were using scripture to justify their ungodly pursuits. Jesus addressed their lack of love and commitment to their wives.

John Gill says, "A man might not dismiss his wife by word of mouth, which might be done hastily, in a passion, of which he might soon repent; but by writing, which was to be drawn up in form; and, before the Sanhedrin in a court procedure, which required time, during which case was finished."

He was then obligated to see that the certificate of divorce was placed in her hand. Gill says, "if he casts a bill to his wife, and she is within the house, or within the court, she is divorced; if he casts it into her bosom, or into her work basket, she is divorced (s):"

Again, Jesus was referring to the Pharisee's hypocritical interpretation of the Mosaic law of divorce and remarriage. The Pharisee's were highly intelligent, skilled students of the law but they were also carnal, hard hearted religious leaders who found a way to use scripture to give themselves permission to fulfill their lusts.

The men we are discussing are divorcing their spouses because they have found younger, prettier women to fulfill their sexual desires. They have clearly violated the marriage covenant.

They are casting divorce decrees upon their wives and abandoning their families. They are robbing them financially without a second thought. Surely, this is not what God had in mind for families.

Chapter 5
God Concedes to Man?

Author Craig S. Keener states in his book "And Marries Another" that God permitted divorce as a concession to human weakness, and with the coming of the Kingdom, God's original plan was being restored.

Can you imagine God conceding to human beings? Yet, I believe this is what Paul was referring to in Acts 17:30 which says, " And the times of this ignorance God winked at; but now commandeth all men everywhere to repent:"

With the coming of God's kingdom within the heart of man via endowment of the Holy Spirit, man would have the power to remain faithfully married to his spouse. Man would have the ability to remain with one wife for the rest of his life.

In the New Testament Paul tells the Corinthians he was not able to communicate with them on an adult level but had to speak to them as if they were children. He also tells them they were behaving as mere men. According to Webster's Dictionary "mere" means nothing more or other than; only, unmixed, pure. To use Webster's definition of unmixed or pure we could say the Corinthians were behaving as pure human beings, not behaving as one mixed or having a combination of both human flesh and Holy Spirit. We are more than fleshly human beings, we are part flesh and part spirit. We are not mere men and women but are a chosen race, a royal priesthood, a dedicated nation, God's own purchased, special people, that you may set forth the wonderful deeds and display the virtues and perfections of Him who called you out of darkness into His marvelous light (1 Peter 2:9).

When Adam and Eve ate the forbidden fruit, their eyes were opened and they noticed they were naked. I wonder if they had not eaten the fruit and had their eyes opened, would a man or woman be sexually attracted to a person that is not their mate? The following verse leads me to believe they would not because that type of attraction is of the world and not of God. 1 John 2:16 says: "For all that is in the world, the lust of the flesh and the lust of the eyes and the vain glory of life, is not of the Father, but is of the world." A man can have a beautiful wife but never be satisfied with her. He still longs for and craves other women. His eyes, lusts and cravings are never satisfied.

He longs for and craves other women to his downfall because scripture tells us he will be judged.

Marriage *is* honorable among all, and the bed undefiled; but fornicators and adulterers God will judge. Hebrews 13:4

Another verse says, an adulterer destroys his own soul.

Whoever commits adultery with a woman lacks understanding; He who does so destroys his own soul. Proverbs 6:32

Chapter 6
Make A Covenant with Your Eyes

In Matthew 5:28 Jesus says if you have a problem with wandering eyes, pluck them out! It is best to enter into heaven with one eye than to go to hell with two. "And if your eye causes you to stumble and sin, pluck it out and throw it away from you; it is better (more profitable and wholesome) for you to enter life with only one eye than to have two eyes and be thrown into the hell (Gehenna) of fire." (Matthew 5:29 Amplified)

Job appears to take Jesus' statement seriously. He did not want to end up in hell because he failed to control his eyes. He said he made a covenant with his eyes not to look lustfully at a girl. We need more covenant making men and women who are determined not to sin against God by sinning with their eyes. The sin of the eyes leads to the culminating act of sexual sin. Our eyes may lead us to the unholy act of joining our bodies to another person, not ordained by God. This can be prevented if we made a covenant with our eyes.

Jobs said, I dictated a covenant (an agreement) to my eyes, how could I look (lustfully) upon a girl?

Job 31:2 For what portion should I have from God above (if I were lewd) and what heritage from the almighty on high?

Job 31:3 Does not calamity (justly) befall the unrighteous and disaster the workers of iniquity?

Job 31:4 Does not (God) see my ways and count all my steps?

Job 31:5 If I have walked with falsehood or vanity, or if my foot has hastened to deceit-

Job 31:6 Oh let me be weighted in a just balance and let Him weigh me, that God may know my integrity!

Job 31:7 If my step has turned out of (God's) way, and my heart has gone the way my eyes (covetously) invited, and if any spot has stained my hands with guilt.

Job 31:8 Then let me sow and let another eat; yes, let the produce of my field or my offspring be rooted out.

When we first read about Job we see that he is the richest man in the country. He has sons and daughters, servants, oxen, donkeys, sheep, and camels. Then one day a strong wind swept in from the desert destroying the house where his children were having a party and killed all of them. A fire came from the sky and killed his servants and all the sheep. Then a group of soldiers came in and took all of his camels and killed the servants that were tending them. Also on the same day, another group of soldiers came in and stole all his oxen and donkeys and killed his servants. Shortly after that terrible day, nasty sores appeared all over his body, covering him from head to toe. His wife began to nag him, saying, "our children are dead, and all of our livestock are gone, which means we don't have a source of income. You have painful, oozing sores covering your body. What's the use in living, you may as well curse God and die, so you don't have to suffer anymore." Instead of cursing God and dying, Job decided to sit on a heap of ashes to examine himself. He said, God, I don't understand why you have allowed these things to happen to me. If I were guilty of lusting after all the girls around town, or if I was some lewd pervert, you would be justified in allowing these terrible things to happen to me. But you know I made a covenant with you, declaring not to look lustfully upon the women I see. I have diligently obeyed you in this area for I know that calamity and disaster fall upon the wicked. Look at my record Lord, I have been determined to live a life of integrity.

In the following verses Job points out that adultery is a heinous crime. A few synonyms for heinous are wicked, evil, satanic and abominable. He said if he had allowed himself to be enticed by a woman or had waited and watched at his neighbor's house and looked for the right time to seduce his neighbor's wife he deserved God's judgment and deserves to be punished.

We know Job's trials were not because of sin and with a clear conscious he could emphatically say it was not because of lust and adultery! It is important to note Job is saying if he were guilty of lusting after women in his heart or committing adultery he deserved the terrible things that happened to him!

If my heart has been deceived and I made a fool by a woman, or if I have (covetously) laid wait at my neighbor's door (until his departure). Then let my wife grind (meal, like a bond slave) for another, and let others bow down upon her.

For (adultery) is a heinous and chief crime, an iniquity (to demand action) by the judges and punishment. (Deuteronomy 22:22; John 8:5) For (uncontrolled passion) is a fire which consumes to Abaddon (to destruction, ruin, and the place of final torment) (that fire once lighted would rage until all is consumed) and would burn to the root of all my (life's increase). Job 31:9-12

Job believed that judgment for the heinous crime of adultery would bring destruction upon his harvest. Throughout scripture we see that when God judges sin, He brings destruction upon the land, especially at harvest time. God gives us two choices: blessings or curses.

Job is referring to Deuteronomy chapter 28 when he speaks of a curse being on the house of the wicked and destruction coming upon his harvest. Let's take a look at what renowned commentator Matthew Henry says about the choices given to us in Deuteronomy chapter 28:

But it shall come to pass, if you do not obey the voice of the Lord your God, to observe carefully all His commandments and His statutes which I command you today, that all these curses will come upon you and overtake you: (Deuteronomy 28:15 NKJV)

Disobeying him, not fulfilling his commandments, or not observing to do them. None fall under his curse but those that rebel against his command. Whatever he does is under a curse too. It is a curse in all that he sets his hand to (Deuteronomy 28:20). A constant disappointment, which those are subject to that set their hearts upon the world. They expect their happiness in it, and which cannot but be a constant vexation. Wherever the sinner goes, the curse of God follows him; wherever he is, it rests upon him. He is cursed in the city and in the field, (Deuteronomy 28:16). The strength of the city cannot shelter him from it, the pleasant air of the country is no fence against these pestilential streams. He is cursed (Deuteronomy 28:19) when he comes in, for the curse is upon the house of the wicked (Proverbs 3:33), and he is cursed when he goes out, for he cannot leave that curse behind him, nor get rid of it, which has entered into his bowels like water and like oil into his bones. (2.) Whatever he has is under a curse: Cursed is the ground for his sake, and all that is on it, or comes out of it, and so he is cursed from the ground, as Cain, (Genesis 4:11).

Compare that to the blessings we receive if we obey.

And all these blessings shall come upon you and overtake you, because you obey the voice of the Lord your God: (Deuteronomy 28:2 NKJV)

We have here the conditions upon which the blessing is promised. It is upon the condition that they diligently hearken to the voice of God (Deuteronomy 28:1,

Deuteronomy 28:2), that they hear God speaking to them by His word, and use their utmost endeavors to acquaint themselves with his will (Deuteronomy 28:13).

Blessed shall you be in the city, and blessed shall you be in the country. (Deuteronomy 28:3 NKJV)

They should be safe and easy; a blessing should rest upon their persons wherever they were, in the city, or in the field (Deuteronomy 28:3). Whether their habitation was in town or country, whether they were husbandmen or tradesmen, whether their business called them into the city or into the field, they should be preserved from the dangers and have the comforts of their condition. This blessing should attend them in their journeys, going out and coming in (Deuteronomy 28:6). Their persons should be protected, and the affair they went about should succeed well. Observe here what a necessary and constant dependence we have upon God both for the continuance and comfort of this life. We need Him at every turn, in all the various movements of life. We cannot be safe if He withdraws His protection, nor is life easy if He suspends His favor. But, if He blesses us, go where we will, it is well with us. Their families should be built up in a numerous issue:

Blessed shall you be when you come in, and blessed shall you be when you go out. (Deuteronomy 28:6 NKJV)

They should have success in all their employments, which would be a constant satisfaction to them: "The Lord shall command the blessing (and it is He only that can command it) upon thee, not only in all thou hast, but in all thou doest, all that thou settest thy hand to," (Deuteronomy 28:8). This intimated that even when they were rich they must not be idle, but must find some good employment or other to set their hand to, and God would own their industry, and bless the work or their hand (Deuteronomy 28:12); for that which makes rich, and keeps so, is the blessing of the Lord upon the hand of the diligent (Proverbs 10:4, and Proverbs 10:22).

Chapter 7
Choices and Consequences

In the book of Deuteronomy God highlights the curses that will come upon those who reject Him and follow the ways of idol worshippers (the world). He said everything they set their hands to do would fail. They would be cursed coming in and going out. Anything they tried to save or store up for the future would be taken by the thief or ruined. They would be cursed with sicknesses, diseases, and poverty. If you read the story of Gideon and the Midianites, you'll find that the Israelites had fallen into idolatry and were being severely oppressed by the Midianites. The Midianites allowed the Israelites to plant their seeds of wheat and barley and raise their cattle. They would then arrive about a month or so before harvest time, set up camp, and raid their fields when it was time to harvest. They took take all of the cattle and all the grain.

We have had several instances of corporations who have allowed their employees to work for many years believing they were saving money for retirement only to have what they worked for all their lives stolen from them at harvest time (retirement). Many worked for years believing they were saving money for their golden years but suddenly their jobs, life savings, and homes were taken from them.

Matthew Henry says, The consequence of God's departure from a people; when He goes all good goes and all mischiefs break in. When Israel kept in with God, they reaped what others sowed (Joshua 24:13; Psalms105:44);

but now that God had forsaken them others reaped what they sowed. Let us take occasion from this to bless God for our national peace and tranquility, that we eat the labor of our hands." (Matthew Henry's Commentary)

In Micah chapter 6, God says He has begun to destroy His people because of their sin. They will store up but save nothing! In Zephaniah chapter 1 God says He will cut off those who bow down and swear to Him and also bow down and swear to Molech (foreign gods).

We are told not to have any other God before or beside Him. That means, you cannot say you love God and obey the god of this world (Satan).

We can't commit adultery and go to church pretending as we have done no wrong.

This *is* the way of an adulterous woman: She eats and wipes her mouth, And says, "I have done no wickedness." (Proverbs 30:20)

God he is sick and tired of people sinning, doing whatever they want to do and going to church acting like that have done no wrong.

He says, Will you steal, murder, commit adultery, swear falsely, burn incense to Baal, and walk after other gods whom you do not know, and *then* come and stand before Me in this house which is called by My name, and say, 'We are delivered to do all these abominations'?(Jeremiah 7:9-10)

The people knew God delivered them from the power of Pharaoh (Satan) and the bondage of Egypt (Sin), however they believed their special relationship with God and his love for them gave them freedom/permission to sin. And so it is today, many believe, since they are "saved" and Jesus died for their sins; they are free to sin because of God's gracious love. However Jude reminds us that God saved/delivered the children of Israel out Egypt (sin) but later destroyed them in the desert because they did not believe him. They did not believe God required "holiness." They were told not commit the same sins as their neighbors. They were not to be fornicators and idolater's as their neighbors were.

'You shall therefore keep all My statutes and all My judgments, and perform them, that the land where I am bringing you to dwell may not vomit you out.
(Leviticus 20:22)

And you shall not walk in the statutes of the nation which I am casting out before you; for they commit all these things, and therefore I abhor them. (Leviticus 20:23)

And so it is today God tells us to separate ourselves from the world in order to inherit the kingdom. (1 Corinthians 6:9-10 and 2 Corinthians 6:15-18)

Although you have accepted Jesus Christ as your Savior, you do not have the freedom to sin (under the license of grace and the ever flowing blood of Jesus). Just as God destroyed the people He delivered from Egypt He will also destroy you if you refuse to repent and believe Him when he says fornicators and adulterers will not enter into the kingdom.

"Blessed *are* those who do His commandments, that they may have the right to the tree of life, and may enter through the gates into the city." (Revelation 22:14)

"But outside *are* dogs and sorcerers and sexually immoral and murderers and idolaters, and whoever loves and practices a lie." (Revelation 22:15)

The Apostle John, said don't be fooled by false teachers who sneakily give you permission to sin under the guise of God's grace and love. They say God loves you sooooo much, that He is not mad at you. I tell you today, that it is possible that God is mad at you!

Scripture tells us "God *is* a just judge, And God is angry *with the wicked* every day." (Psalms 7:11)

Although you may be in the midst of sin and all is going well physically and financially, it doesn't mean God is pleased with you or your behavior nor is He excusing it. He's giving you time to repent. Many think because judgment is delayed they are getting away with their sin but they are not for the day judgment is sure to come as the rising of tomorrow's sun. For there is a set day, a day God has determined to punish the wicked.

The LORD has made all for Himself, Yes, even the wicked for the day of doom. (Proverbs 16:4)

For the wicked are reserved for the day of doom; They shall be brought out on the day of wrath. (Job 21:30)

Our Choices and Our Children

The children of Israel adopted the custom of sacrificing their children to Molech. One may say a man or woman has sacrificed his or her child to this unknown god by forsaking them to pursue fleshly lusts. The children become burned by the flames of their parents adulterous relationships. Many children are scarred for life never to recover from their parents lack of self-control. Again, this should not occur among those redeemed and ransomed from the fall.

Children are often forgotten, and made to feel unwanted. They feel that they are the cause of their parent's divorce. It's not uncommon for a man to divorce his wife for a much younger wife. Sometimes the new wife doesn't want her husband to have anything to do with his past, requiring him to stop having contact with his children. The new wife wants all of his attention. The children don't understand why their dad no longer wants to see them. They wonder why he left their mother and never looked back. Many children become angry and have a difficult time resuming a relationship with their father once he awakens from the fog of deception.

Do we ever stop and think about our choices and how they affect us and everyone around us? Do we realize that we are also turning our backs on God? He is the one who loves us above all. He created us to have an everlasting relationship with Him. Let's choose eternal life instead of temporary pleasures.

Chapter 8
Decide to Forgive and Trust Again

If infidelity has entered into your marriage, you have a couple of decisions to make. Can you get past this and forgive your spouse? Scripture tells us to, "Bear with each other and forgive whatever grievances you may have against one another. Forgive as the Lord forgave you. And over all these virtues put on love, which binds them all together in perfect unity." (Colossians 3:13-14)

Once a person has cheated it is hard to trust that person again. The person responsible for breaking their vows will be required to develop the patience of Job if they want to keep their marriage together. The other spouse will question them: Where were you? Why did it take you so long to go to the store? Were you really working late? Why did that person hang up the phone when I answered it? You may find your spouse checking your cell phone, your computer, your calendar, or going through your belongings. If you do not have anything to hide, he or she will not find anything. You are going to have to endure it without complaining. This is one way to win back their trust. Start complimenting your spouse, surprising him or her with small gifts, and letting that person know they mean more to you than anyone else. The spouse who was wronged needs to remember that no one is perfect. Jesus is the only sinless person. Notice that he or she is making an effort. Praise them when they make you happy. Remember to "Be kind and compassionate to one another,

forgiving each other, just as Christ God forgave you."
(Ephesians 4:32)

Many couples choose to stay together only to end up filing
for a divorce later because they could/would not forgive
their partner. However, in order to avoid making a rash
decision, it is possible to separate for a time to heal and
then come together again after counseling. During this
time it is possible to learn to date and get to know one
another. Learning to forgive in such a time is a beautiful
reminder of God's magnificent grace towards us. He
forgave our infidelity when we walked after the flesh in
various means, the apostle Paul said, Now the works of the
flesh are manifest, which are these; adultery, fornication,
uncleanness, lasciviousness, idolatry, witchcraft, hatred,
variance, emulations, wrath, strife, seditions, heresies,
envyings, murders, drunkenness, revellings... (Galatians
5:20-21). Let's forgive like our Lord who said "forgive and
you will be forgiven." (Luke 6:37)

If you plan to follow God and redeem your marriage you
may need outside support. Support can take the form of
someone you can lean on, but it should be someone who
will remind you of God's will and plans for your life. It
should be someone that will bring you back to God's
words if your mind begins to wander and doubt the
possibility of a successful restoration of your marriage.
You will also need your Church family behind you. "For
where there are two or three gathered together in my
name, there am I in the midst of them." (Matthew 18:20)
Imagine the whole Church encouraging you and praying

for you. You will need to diligently seek God and ask Him for wisdom. Ask Him to fill you with love. Ask Him to remove any bitterness or resentment from your heart and He will gladly come to your aid.

Commit to overcoming this assault on your marriage and be counted among the victors noted in the bible. Christ gives kudos to those who overcome the difficult challenges in this life (Revelation 21:7). Hebrews chapter 11 notes the men and women who obtained God's precious promises in the midst of trying circumstances. From being able to bear children in old age to turning one's back on untold riches, status and position in order to obey God's will. Strive to be counted among the cloud of witnesses who are cheering you on as you run your race. You can do it, go for the golden crown!

References

Expat. (n.d.) In Wikipedia. Retrieved from
https://en.wikipedia.org/wiki/Expatriate

Divorce Statics in America. Retrieved from
http://www.divorcestatistics.org/

Retrieved from
http://www.biblestudytools.com/commentaries/gills-
exposition-of-the-bible/proverbs-2-17.html

Retrieved from
http://www.biblestudytools.com/commentaries/gills-
exposition-of-the-bible/deuteronomy-24-1.html

Retrieved from
http://bible.wiktel.com/mhc/deuteronomy/28.html

www.ingramcontent.com/pod-product-compliance
Lightning Source LLC
Chambersburg PA
CBHW060949050426
42337CB00052B/3289